What Can I Make Today?

I Can Make a
Truck

Joanna Issa

Raintree is an imprint of Capstone Global Library Limited, a company incorporated in England and Wales having its registered office at 7 Pilgrim Street, London, EC4V 6LB – Registered company number: 6695582

Edited by Penny West
Designed by Philippa Jenkins
Picture research by Elizabeth Alexander
Originated by Capstone Global Library Ltd
Production by Victoria Fitzgerald
Printed and bound in China

ISBN 978 1 406 28405 8
18 17 16 15 14
10 9 8 7 6 5 4 3 2 1

British Library Cataloguing in Publication Data
A full catalogue record for this book is available from the British Library.

Acknowledgements
We would like to thank Capstone Publishers/ © Karon Dubke for permission to reproduce photographs.

Cover photograph reproduced with permission of Capstone Publishers/ © Karon Dubke.

We would like to thank Philippa Jenkins for her invaluable help in the preparation of this book.

Every effort has been made to contact copyright holders of material reproduced in this book. Any omissions will be rectified in subsequent printings if notice is given to the publishers.

Disclaimer
All the Internet addresses (URLs) given in this book were valid at the time of going to press. However, due to the dynamic nature of the Internet, some addresses may have changed, or sites may have changed or ceased to exist since publication. While the author and Publishers regret any inconvenience this may cause readers, no responsibility for any such changes can be accepted by either the author or the Publishers.

Contents

Some words are shown in bold, like this. You can find them in the glossary on page 23.

What do I need to make a truck?

To make the cab and **trailer**, you will need a large box, a small box that's the same width as the large box, card, a split pin, double-sided sticky tape, masking tape, a pencil and scissors.

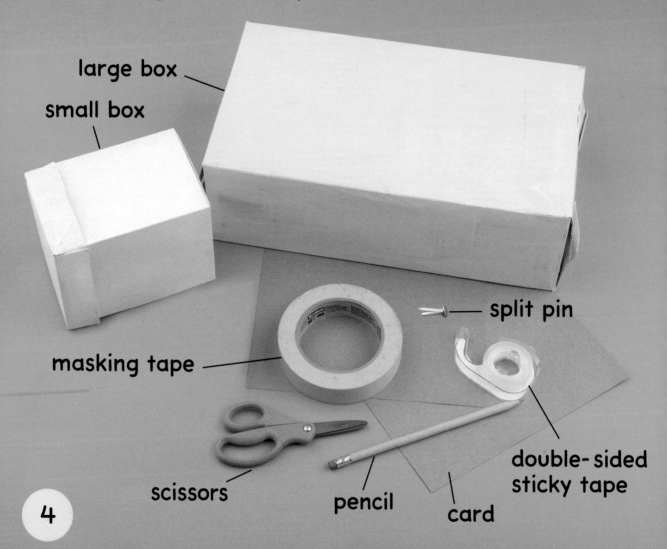

large box

small box

split pin

masking tape

double-sided sticky tape

scissors

pencil

card

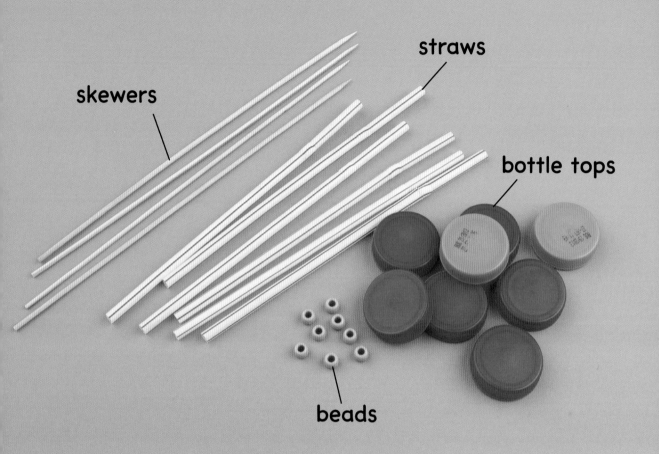

skewers

straws

bottle tops

beads

To make the wheels and **axles**, you will need four **skewers**, eight beads with a large enough hole for a skewer, six straws and eight bottle tops.

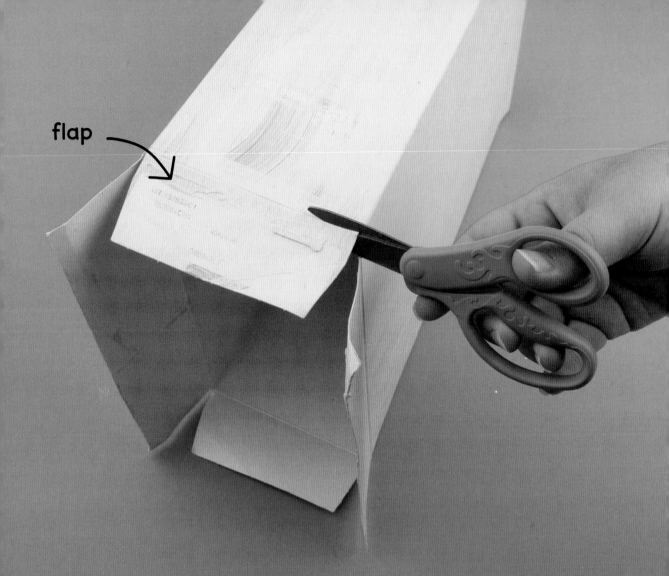

flap

Make the trailer

Use the large box to make the
trailer. To make the trailer
ramp, open one end of the large
box and cut off the top flap.

Cut a rectangle of card so it is the same width and height as the end of the large box. Stick it to the bottom flap of the box with masking tape.

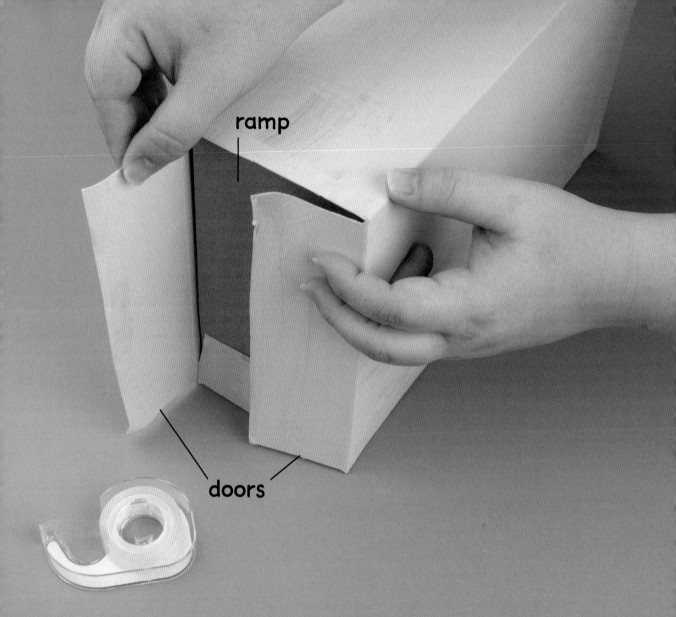

ramp

doors

To close the doors, push the **ramp** up, then use double-sided sticky tape to secure the doors.

Make the cab

Use the small box to make the cab. To make the front window, draw a rectangle on one of the wide sides of the box. Next, make the side windows. Draw a square on each of the narrow sides of the box. Then ask an adult to help you cut out the shapes.

Ask for adult help

front window

Lift the lid of the small box to make the roof of the cab.

To fix the cab to the **trailer**, cut a rectangle from card. It should be 10 centimetres longer than the cab. Stick double-sided sticky tape to one end of the rectangle.

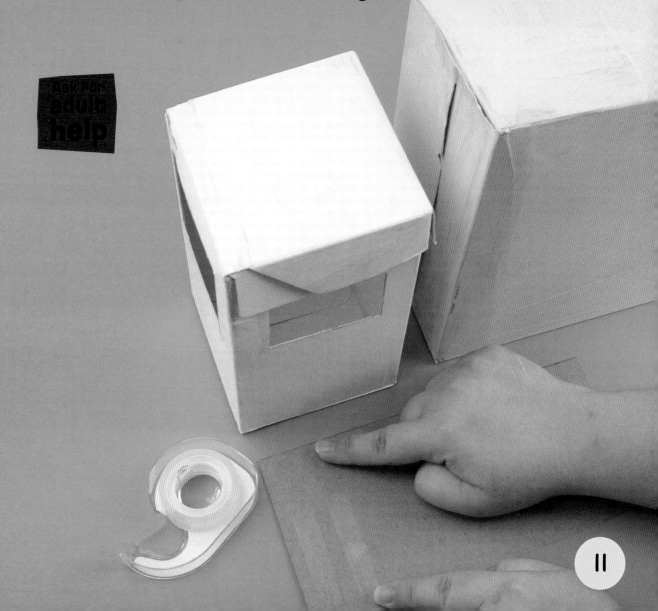

Ask for adult help

Stick the cab on to the card.

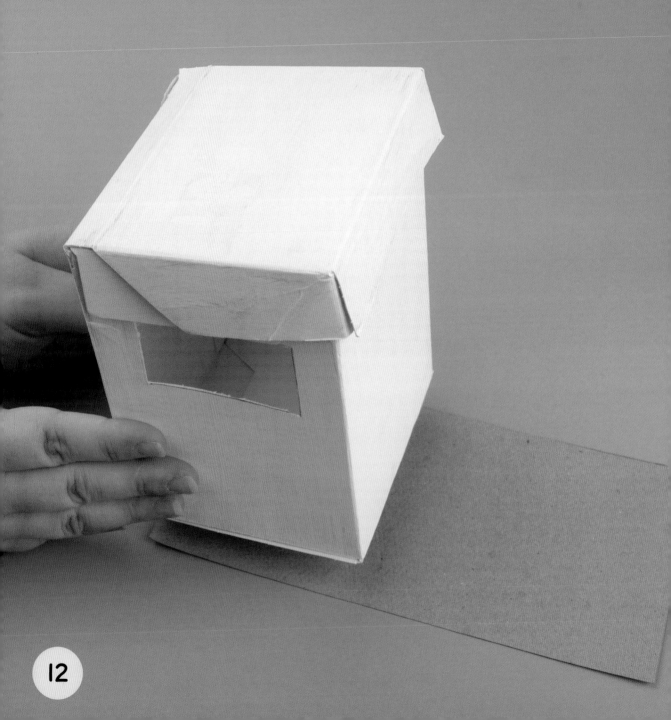

Make a hole in the end of the card with the split pin.

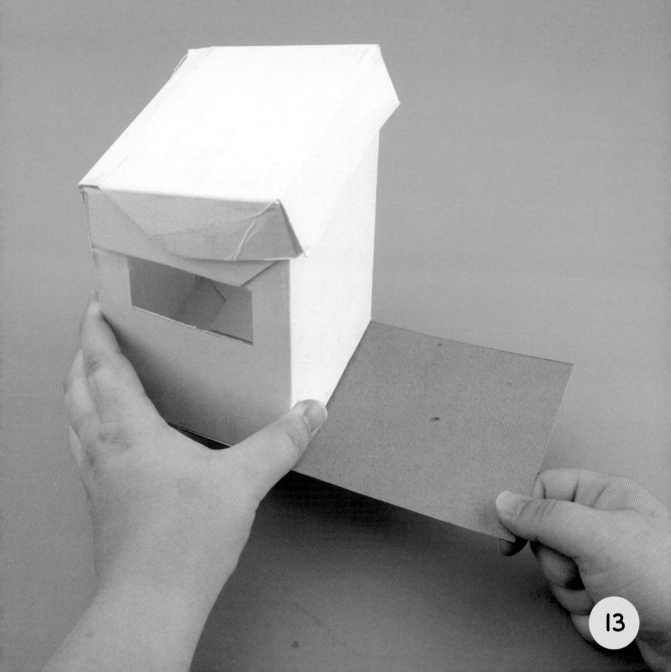

Make a hole in the **trailer** with
the split pin. Leave a small space
between the cab and the trailer.
Push a split pin through the holes to
fix the trailer to the card.

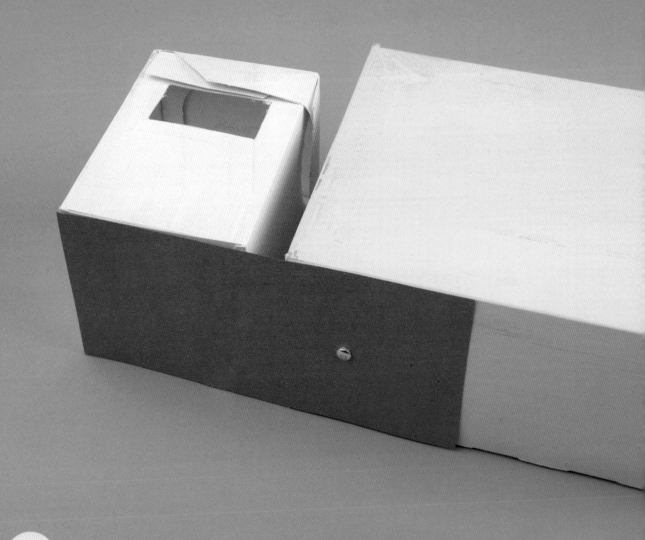

Make the axles

Cut four straws a little wider than the truck. Tape three straws underneath the trailer and one straw underneath the cab.

Cut the wooden **skewers** so they are 2 centimetres longer than the straws.

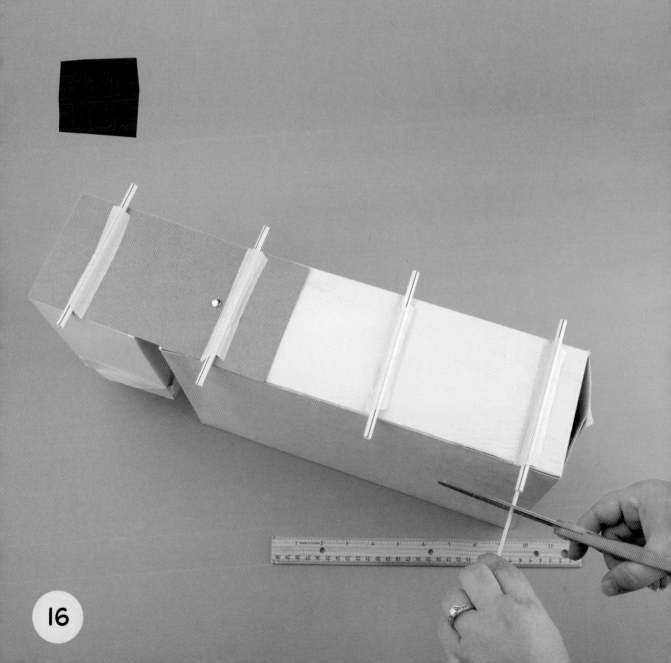

Push the skewers inside the straws.

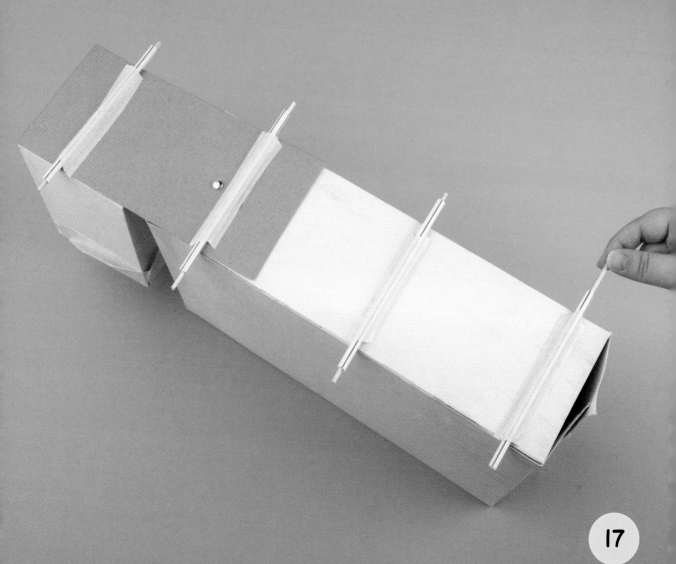

Make the wheels

Ask an adult to make a hole in each bottle top. Each hole should be wide enough to fit onto a **skewer**.

Ask for adult help

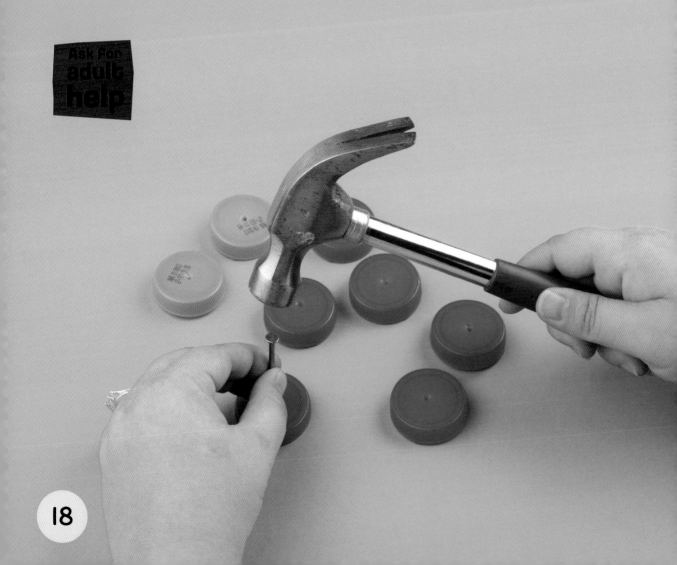

Push a bottle top onto the end of
each wooden skewer. Stick a small
piece of double-sided sticky tape
around the end of the skewer.

Push the bead on to hold it in place.
Do this for all the wheels.

Stick a straw to each side of the cab. You have finished your truck! You can decorate it with paint or coloured paper if you like.

What can you make today?

You could make a truck and **trailer** as a gift for Father's Day or a birthday present.

Picture glossary

axle long stem that the wheels are attached to

ramp flat part of the trailer that can be lowered or raised

skewer thin stick used to hold pieces of food together

trailer part of the truck that is towed by the cab

Find out more

Books

Machines on the Road (Machines at Work), Sian Smith (Raintree, 2013)

Make It!, Jane Bull (Dorling Kindersley, 2013)

Wheels and Axles (How Toys Work), Sian Smith (Raintree, 2012)

Websites

www.bbc.co.uk/cbeebies/presenters/makes
On this website, you will find craft projects to do.

www.thecraftycrow.net
Visit this website to read about fun art activities.

Index